TELLING A CHILD
ABOUT DEATH

Books by EDGAR N. JACKSON

TELLING
A
CHILD
ABOUT
DEATH

by *EDGAR N. JACKSON*

HAWTHORN BOOKS, INC.
W. Clement Stone, Publisher
NEW YORK

Library of Congress Catalog Card Number: 65-21676
ISBN: 0-8015-7494-3

8 9 10

Contents

TELLING A CHILD
ABOUT DEATH

I . *The Importance of the Task*

SOMETIMES adults try to spare children the necessity of facing tragic circumstances. When there is a difference of opinion among adults in the family, they try to settle the matter without letting the children overhear the argument. When there is a financial crisis, they try to resolve the problem without worrying the child. When a neighborhood crisis develops, they seek to cope with it without letting the child become aware of it. When serious illness develops, they are apt to play it down as far as the youngsters are concerned. This protective attitude toward children's sensibilities is quite a natural trait among adults, and wisely so, for it is difficult to expect children to think or act like adults.

But insofar as the tragic circumstances of death are a part of the emotional experience of life, it is difficult to exclude children completely from some awareness of them. Because children are particularly sensitive to changes in the emotional climate, they tend to be aware of things in general even if they do not understand things in particular. When something goes wrong in the family, they are apt to ask, "Daddy, what's the matter with mommy?" Sooner or later they will show that they know there is something wrong, even though they may not know what it is. It is hard to keep secrets from children, for they overhear things that are said or they observe differences in the family routine. They find their security in routines that are taken for granted. When change occurs, they are apt to be quick to sense it.

If children do not find a real explanation to fit what they sense or overhear, they may let their imaginations run wild. They may assume that Daddy doesn't love Mother any more. This would be a much more disturbing thing to cope with than the simple fact that there is a difference of opinion. They may even assume that they are to blame for changes in attitudes in the family, and this can threaten their security where it is most important. They are so completely enmeshed in family life that any modifications of it can cause deep distress and anxiety.

Adult behavior is often baffling to children. Loud talk in the quiet of the night when it is assumed that they are sleeping is often frightening to children. Quiet talk from which they are excluded may have the same effect. When they ask, "What are you talking about?" and get the answer, "Oh, nothing," they know it is not an answer but an evasion, and their imagination goes to work. Because their lives are so bound up with strong feelings, the imagination is apt to use a mixture of much fancy and few facts and come up with some rather weird interpretations of relatively simple events.

These weird interpretations don't seem out of keeping to the child whose limited facts get mixed with strong feelings. Six-year-old Freddy overheard a conversation between his mother and his grandmother, who had come for a visit. Freddy thought that his grandparents were tops and would stay a long time. When he heard his grandmother say, "I guess we had forgotten what small children are like. We have decided a short visit is better than a longer one," Freddy immediately concluded that his grandparents were leaving ahead of schedule because they did not like him. He had recently learned that a child in his neighborhood was adopted. His limited logic concluded that his grandparents did not like him because he was not really their grandchild but was adopted. His enthusiasm turned to quiet dismay. His parents could not understand why his usual behavior had changed so rapidly.

A day or two after the grandparents had left, his mother said to Freddy, "What's the matter? Do you miss your grandparents?" His mother was surprised to hear him blurt out, "Why didn't you tell me I'm not really your little boy?" When she answered, "Why, Freddy, where did you ever get such an outlandish idea?" he burst into tears, and they were able to get to the bottom of his strong feelings that had been attached to a couple of random and unrelated facts. Only then was the matter talked out and Freddy properly reassured.

Because in the early years of their lives children live

mostly by strong feelings of love and disappointment, security and insecurity, anger and apprehension, they are sensitive to the emotional meanings they attach to the things that are said and done around them. It is much safer to be doubly careful to make sure that they understand the meanings of events as they experience them than to leave them to their own devices as far as interpretation and imagination are concerned.

Children seem to have built-in lie detectors, but the sensitivity of their detection is bound up with feelings more than facts, for their experience in factual events is limited but the depth of their sensitivity to feelings is almost unlimited.

So the child knows when something important has happened in his small world. He may not be sure what it means, and his efforts to find meanings are often quite damaging to him. It is better to supply him with the simple facts, no matter how distressing they may be, than to leave him on his own in seeking meanings. Sooner or later the truth will out, for few family secrets are well kept. Our only alternative is to help the child meet events with honesty and good sense.

Once when I was speaking to a parent-teacher group on this subject, one of the parents responded by saying, "There will be plenty of time for my children to face life's unpleasantness when they grow older. I am going to shield mine as long as I can." At first this seems like a commendable sentiment. But, unfortunately, it does not take into account the simple fact that the child does not live in a world completely controlled by his parents. He turns to them for security in finding meanings for the new events that stretch his past experience. If he cannot find reasonable answers from his parents he will look elsewhere, or he may turn inward for answers that he is poorly equipped to give.

Sometimes the questions he needs answers for have to do with the death of a neighbor or a pet, or the meaning of new words he has heard used that open up the matter of tragic events he has heard about but cannot explain. Realistically, death in some form or other is all about, and it is false to try to ignore its existence. To deny a child a reasonable interpretation of the events he hears about as they happen is to deprive him of parental insight and reassurance when he needs it most. We cannot live in a make-believe world where unpleasantness does not exist. The need to learn how to meet deprivation comes early in life, and the calm, assured facing of it can help the child to grow in understanding at the same time that his experience is widening.

Bob's parents faced this task unexpectedly but used it for good educational purposes. Bob was thrilled when he received a card from his uncle in Arizona saying that he was sending the boy a horned toad. Bob got his book of animal facts and read all he could find out about these little creatures. When he read that they enjoyed hot sand, he built a small pen, filled it with sand, and put it in the sun to make a desertlike spot in New York. A few days later a cigar box arrived with the horned toad, but the toad would not move. Bob took it out and nudged it with his finger. He put it on the sand to see if it would move. His mother said, "Maybe it is dazed from the long trip in a cigar box." Bob watched hour after hour, but no sign of life appeared.

When his father came home from the office that evening, Bob asked many questions about the toad and its behavior. "It couldn't be still that long, could it?" he asked. His father told him he was sure the toad was dead. He pointed out that the long journey by mail probably was more than it could endure. Bob was disappointed because he had made many plans for his toad. He was going to take him to school to show his teacher. He was going to invite his friends in to see the unusual creature. Now he had to change his plans. He asked his father, "What do you do with a dead horned toad?" His father suggested that they wrap it up in paper and bury it. This was done.

Bob continued to talk about the pet he had almost had. His father, well aware that this was Bob's first direct encounter with death, wanted to drain the experience of emotional hazard. Yet he didn't want to dwell on it unreasonably. The more Bob talked, the less he dwelt upon his disappointment and the more he seemed to like the suggestion that some day they would take a trip to Arizona where they could see horned toads as they live naturally. He fitted the experience into his emotional needs and native curiosity and grew through both to a healthy attitude toward something we humans all have to take into account. He was building an idea of death as a natural process, ever present in nature, often disappointing, but something that people learn to cope with.

No child lives in an emotional vacuum. Things keep happening to him. His world is enmeshed in strong feelings. The good feelings he wants to repeat. The unpleasant ones he wants to get away from as much as possible. When things happen that are quite painful, he reacts by retreating into a world he makes more comfortable by his defenses. Some of these may be quite simple. When he wants to put something in his mouth and there is no food handy, he may stick his thumb in as a substitute. When he is corrected by his parents for some unacceptable behavior, he may get angry and say, "Boy, when I grow up you won't do that to me." He enters a world of the future. He may threaten to run away, and even though he does not do it, he enjoys thinking about the idea of asserting his freedom. When he is faced with a big problem, he may develop a big escape and may wander far into the realm of fanciful thoughts. What he is trying to do is to match his ideas of escape with the size of the threat that he experiences.

Some of his escapes may be healthy and useful. He may go out to play and through the use of his large muscle systems work out his excess energy. Some of his escapes may become a hazard that increases with the years. If he retreats from the unpleasant facts of life by trying to live in an unreal world, he may make it difficult to keep clear distinctions between what is real and what is make-believe.

A fear of death that makes one run away from the fact is little protection against a recurring reality, so it is a poor defense. But understanding that removes fear and helps one to grow through the disappointments is a useful defense against the injuring aspects of experience. When the early experiences of life are wisely handled, they help to build the sound understanding that makes life secure.

Everyone has to learn to accept some things and get along without others. Every time we make a choice, we have to decide that we want one thing enough to deprive ourselves of the other. "Would you rather go to the beach or to the zoo?" The problem of alternatives is always with us. The earlier a child learns to accept some forms of deprivation as essential to life, the sooner he builds a special kind of strength into his life. Learning to get along without some things in order to have others that are judged more important is a long step toward the kind of wisdom that is an ingredient of true happiness. The earlier he learns this, the more emotional strength he finds for his life.

Studies of child behavior show that when the fact of death is not well handled by adults, the child may be deeply injured. Often this shows itself not so much by what is said as by what is done. The child is often quite limited in his verbal ability, but his behavior becomes a quick and spontaneous way of communicating what is going on inside of him. Sometimes even the behavior is difficult to interpret. One study of so-called juvenile delinquency points out that many children who engaged in destructive behavior were showing that their grief was mixed with strong feelings of anger against life. This usually shows that the events surrounding the tragic experience had not been properly interpreted. The child had used imagination and magical thinking to give a meaning to the events that was damaging to him.

We saw how imagination can work in the illustration of Freddy and his thoughts about adoption. Magical thinking is similar in its results but different in its origin. Young children have very little experience in using ideas or thoughts. They know that if they ask for something, they usually get it. They may easily get the idea that if they think a thought, it is the same as doing the act. They may say, "I hope it doesn't rain." It doesn't rain. They can assume that it was their expressed hope that actually controlled the weather. Usually, experience with the uncontrollable nature of the weather finally corrects such magical trends in thinking. But the roots of the magical thinking, and the feelings of omnipotence that go with it, are present to some degree in the mental life of every child.

If a child cries out in anger against an adult and says, "I wish you were dead," he does not know the full meaning of his words, but he may well feel overwhelmed by his feelings about the magical power of his words if shortly thereafter that adult should die. He quite naturally feels that it is his fault. He blames himself for what has happened. He may want to punish himself for thinking the thoughts that he feels have brought such disastrous results. So he may deliberately do things that he knows will cause punishment. This may be his way of working out his guilty feelings. Or the painful feelings may be pushed out of consciousness and in a roundabout way come back to determine his behavior, so that without really planning it he does things to satisfy this unconscious need to be punished.

In one study of child behavior over 75 per cent of the children who had serious problems so far as their social behavior was concerned had suffered the loss of a parent in the early years of life. Their actions had become a way of showing their anger and resistance to what they felt was unjust. What they needed had been taken from them. Their actions showed their resentment at being deprived. At times the anger was turned inward and they did things to invite punishment. At other times it was turned outward as they fought against the world around them which they felt had hurt them. You have seen a child spontaneously kick at or strike some inanimate object that he felt had injured him. The same reaction can follow as he strikes out against an environment he does not understand very well but which he personifies as the cause of his intolerable injury. Of course, he does not deliberately say, "I will injure society because it injured me." Rather, his damaged feelings make it difficult for him to live wisely in the world around him, and his injured feelings show up in destructive behavior. Sometimes this happens in ways that are unexpected, and the underprivileged may often be the emotionally deprived rather than the materially impoverished.

Children think their parents are all-powerful. Little children are confused when a parent cannot meet a crisis with complete mastery. Ellen's father was a physician. When her mother became ill, she told her small friends, "My father won't let my mother die. He is a good doctor." When Ellen's mother did die of an inoperable malignancy, it was easier for her to feel anger against her father than to feel normal grief for her mother. She turned against her father and cried, "You did it. You are a bad man." Her father, distraught with weeks of incessant vigil, was not able to handle Ellen's emotions wisely. He scolded her for her words and punished her for her actions. This verified her feelings of anger against her father.

When father and daughter needed each other most, they were separated by their inability to understand that anger is a part of grief. The difficulty could have been resolved if, instead of scolding, her father had been able to say, "Ellen, I know how you must feel. There are times when we are all weak and inadequate. More than anything else in my life, I wanted to restore your mother to health. But I failed. I didn't know enough. I'm so sad I can't find words to tell you how I feel."

Because Ellen's anger was a deep and irrational emotion, her father would have had to tell her in many ways over a long period of time how he felt and how he understood her feelings. But when he added his anger to hers and rejected her feelings, she was further injured by the one she would normally have turned to for understanding. Her grief left not only a sense of shattering personal loss but also unresolved anger that showed up in unexpected places in irrational behavior for years to come.

But the injured emotion does not always show itself in angry behavior. In the child guidance center with which I was associated, the grief of a child was sometimes revealed in an emotional disturbance that made it difficult for him to get along with others, to make progress in school, or to have proper feelings about himself.

In one case the father of a young boy died suddenly of a heart ailment. When no one would answer his questions about the event, by a strange twist of reasoning he assumed he was the cause. Like most boys he had misbehaved and knew his misbehavior had displeased his father. He saw his action as the cause of his father's death, and he could not tolerate the feelings of guilt that overcame him. He became so preoccupied with these emotions that he could not do his school work, became withdrawn and listless at home, and in truth became a seriously ill youngster emotionally. It took careful treatment to help him work through his feelings and see that he was not the cause and could live free of that guilt. Had the matter been handled better at the very beginning, he would have been spared these months of emotional pain.

A similar event was handled more wisely in the life of Johnny, whose father also died of a heart ailment. Johnny's mother was so distraught that she felt she could not talk as calmly as she wished, so she asked her pastor to talk with her son. Johnny seemed confused and uncertain. On his next visit to the home the pastor talked with Johnny alone. His opening question was:

"Johnny, do you understand what happened to your father?"

Johnny replied, "He just died, I guess."

The pastor asked, "Do you know what that means?"

Johnny said, "Not really, I guess."

After a pause the pastor said, "There are some things about dying that puzzle us all, but perhaps I can help you understand some of them. Is there anything you would like to talk with me about?"

Immediately Johnny asked, "Why did my father have to die?"

The pastor explained, "The doctor told me your father had an illness when he was young that weakened his heart. His heart would not stand the strain that was put on it, and it stopped pumping blood. When that happened, he was dead."

"Yes, I know about the heart," Johnny said. "But I still don't understand why it had to happen to him."

"How do you mean, Johnny?" the pastor asked.

"Do you think I caused the strain?" Johnny blurted out.

"No, Johnny, I don't think you did," the pastor said. "In fact, I think the opposite was true. Your father loved you so much and you brought such great joy to his life that I'm sure you were good for him and for his heart."

Johnny looked searchingly into the pastor's eyes as if to be sure he could believe what he had heard, and then he said quietly, "Do you think I could have done anything to keep him from dying?"

"That would be hard to know," the pastor said. "We can always think of things we could have done differently, but we cannot go back into the past and do things over. We do the best we know how in the present, and let that stand. I am sure you were always a good son, and I know your father loved and valued you. Even when he scolded you for your mischief, he knew it was your boyish nature and he loved it. He always wanted the best possible life for you."

The pastor's main purpose was to give reassurance to Johnny about the circumstances of his father's death and especially about his father's love for him. This was essential to relieve any doubts and fears that might build up into strong guilt feelings.

To a ten-year-old child the assurance of an adult has deep meaning. He can build on it. The pastor left the way open for Johnny to talk with him whenever he wanted to, for the loneliness of a child for his father can cause recurring doubts and fears. It is important that he have a place where he can find reassurance and an understanding adult who will talk with him whenever the need exists. Some ideas have to be repeated many times before they seep into the lower levels of consciousness where emotions hold sway, and this would be especially true of the ideas related to a boy's feelings for his father.

Sometimes adults have an unreasonable fear of death. They avoid funerals and cannot talk with persons who are mourning. On careful examination, these feelings can often be traced back to a time in childhood when the pain of loss was not wisely cared for. As the years went by, the feelings of apprehension and fear grew, until as adults they felt helpless to cope with them. This is a shaky basis to build on in the face of events that are bound to affect all of us sooner or later.

It doesn't have to be that way. The emotional crises of life can be used to teach wise response to deprivation and loss. When emotionally painful events are faced honestly, the pain is drained out and does not attach itself to the future.

More than we realize, the failure of our culture grows from our failure to wisely meet problems of life and death. We make light of death in television Westerns and gangster gunplay, and then are poorly equipped to deal with the real thing when we have to. When we are face to face with major crises in our era, such as the threat posed by the cold war, the possibility of atomic warfare, and intercontinental missiles, we cannot really take hold of the problems with competence because we cannot think of death realistically, and continue to live in the make-believe world that affirms, "It can't happen to me," or "Let's sweep the unpleasant things under the carpet and go on with our whistling."

Until we develop a sounder approach to death, we cannot have a well-balanced philosophy of life. There can be no better way to start the task of building more solid foundations for a philosophy of life than by honestly and wisely facing the questions children ask when they have their first encounters with acute loss. It is not a matter of getting around these difficult questions as quickly and easily as possible. Rather, it is important to recognize and accept the opportunity they afford to teach some of life's most significant lessons.

2. *When to Talk About Death*

OFTEN parents ask, "When should you talk about death with a child?" Although it may seem to oversimplify the matter, the answer is, "When the child wants to talk about it." The events that can raise the question are happening regularly. Sometimes the child seems unaware of them and at other times appears to have a morbid curiosity concerning them. Children differ widely in their ability to form questions. They react differently to question-raising events. Often their approach to any given question is conditioned by the way previous questions have been met.

If you are apprehensive you may show your emotion by trying to overanswer a question, as well as by trying to divert or ignore it. Sooner or later, in one way or another, directly or indirectly, the question about death is inevitable. Like most important questions, it grows out of the experience of daily living.

An airliner crashes and the newscaster says, "One hundred and six persons perished in a jet crash." The child asks, "What is 'parish'?" The principal comes into the first grade and asks to speak to the teacher alone. She comes back into the room a few minutes later with tears in her eyes and tells her class, "I have just received word that my father is very sick and may die. I must go home for a few days." The first-grade teacher is an important figure in her pupils' lives. They identify with her feelings. They will take the emotion they saw in their teacher's eyes and attach it to the event of dying. Questions will inevitably be raised, and answers will be needed. An automobile accident, the death of an aged relative or of a neighbor, will bring the fact of death into the child's world. It will need to be met at the point where it arises.

The questions will vary. They may show the limited understanding of the child but they will also show the quality of his feelings. It is this quality of feeling that is the important starting point in approachng an answer.

As your child works to tie the unusual event to his past experience, he may ask, "Why did my teacher cry?" "What do you do when you die?" "Where do dead people go?" "How do you go to the bathroom when you are dead?" Or he may show that he has made the experience more personal by asking, "When are you going to die?" or saying, "I don't want to be dead."

Usually the inevitable question is related to an inevitable event. We may be prepared for it, or we may be surprised. However it is, it is important to make sure we know what the child has in mind before giving an answer. There is little purpose in answering questions that aren't asked. We must guard against confusing our adult meanings for words with those the child has in mind.

Workmen come to cut down a dead tree. The child, very much interested in the whole process, asks, "Why are those men cutting down my tree?" You would naturally answer, "That tree is dead." This invites the further question, "When is a tree dead?" It gives an opportunity to point out to the child that the dead tree has no leaves and its bark is falling off. This fact is compared with facts about other trees whose leaves are blowing in the breeze. There is a factual difference between being dead and being alive. This simple fact may be all that is needed for an answer. It becomes part of the basic equipment for understanding why death is different from life. It is honest, it is related to the simple events, and it has met the child's question where it was raised.

Your child may come in from play carrying a dead bird. With no special feeling of the state of the bird, he may say, "Look, I caught a bird." When he had chased birds before they had flown away. This one was different. He had it in his hand. You may casually examine the bird and say, "This little bird is dead. It won't fly any more."

The child may then say, "Why won't it?" This question shows that he does not understand all that is meant by the first explanation. He wants to know more. Then you may say, "A dead bird is not like a bird that is alive. A live bird can fly, and eat the bird seed we put out for it. A dead bird can't fly or eat ever again." The answer is honest and adequate for the question asked. The next question will show whether or not it is all he wants to know. He may then say, "What shall I do with it?" It follows naturally to say, "I'll get a little box, you dig a hole over there, and we'll bury it." This may bring another question. "Why should we bury it?" The answer may well be, "When little birds die they don't need their bodies any more, so we bury them where they are safe from harm." With the activity of the burial the event will probably be closed and play will be resumed. When another event involving death and burial occurs, he has had some preparation at his level of comprehension, and he approaches the new experience without fear because no fear was engendered in the event now past.

Sometimes the stories we tell children raise the question of death. Traditional stories do not hesitate to mention it, but it is usually a type of death that does not make the child feel uncomfortable. Generations of children were told of Jack, the Giant Killer without suffering emotional injury, because they felt as if they were Jack rather than the giant. Not every event that depicts death has an equal emotional impact upon a child. It is important to be sensitive to the child's feelings as he uses the words and tries to develop a meaning for them.

For most children the first encounter with death in

the family comes through the death of a grandparent. Grandparents have a special place in the emotional life of their grandchildren, for they represent affection and an indulgence that is treasured. How can the death of so important a person in the child's life be explained and made acceptable to a child? No two family situations are quite the same, but the following experiences show a constructive and a destructive way of explaining an event to a grandchild.

Susan lived in a large city. Her grandparents lived on a farm. For Susan nothing was more interesting than a trip to the farm. Everything was alive and moving, and her grandfather was in charge of it all. He enjoyed his granddaughter so much that he spent hours with her watching the little pigs, riding a pony, and feeding baby chicks. She basked in the excitement of the farm and her grandfather's love. When word came that her grandfather was seriously ill with a kidney infection, Susan, her parents, and her little brother went at once to the farm. For several days she was aware of the critical condition of her grandfather. She saw him a few times, and even to an eight-year-old child it was obvious that he was very sick. When he died, the simple and open honesty of rural people dealt with his death sorrowfully but candidly. Neighbors talked to Susan about her grandfather. No limits were placed on conversation or questions. Susan asked to go to the funeral in the little village church. She did not understand all that was said, but she felt a part of it.

The meaning of the sad days and their events were summed up in a conversation her father overheard when Susan was explaining to four-year-old Richard the changes that had taken place. As they watched the little pigs eating their supper, she said, "Your grandpa is dead. That means he won't be here any more. He won't milk the cows. He won't feed the pigs. So if there is anything you want to know, you'll have to ask me." She accepted the fact, she accepted its meaning, and she accepted her responsibility in the new state of affairs death had caused. The circumstances were honest and open, and her reaction was direct and un-complicated. While she would not forget her grand-father, she was not emotionally damaged by his death.

In the same community lived another girl named Susan, but we will call her Sue for short. She was eight also, and within a year had an experience of death quite different from our other Susan. Sue's grandfather had lived with the family for several years. He did not hear well, so people yelled at him to make him hear. Sue always thought people were angry when they yelled. Her grandfather died unexpectedly and at night. His body was removed before Sue awoke in the morning. Her parents decided that the less said about his death the better. They thought Sue was too young to understand such things. Because most of his friends were either dead or far away, a private service was planned. When Sue asked at breakfast where her grandfather was, her father said he had a sick spell but she shouldn't worry, because everything would be all right. Sue went to school as usual. A couple of days later a private service was conducted while Sue was at school. She had felt that something strange was going on, but when her questions were dodged, she stopped asking. She was hardly prepared for the encounter that took place at school.

John, a classmate, said, "I'm sorry your grandfather died."

Sue, baffled and uncertain, said sharply, "He did not."

John, somewhat uncertain, said, "He did too. My mother said so."

Sue only repeated, "He did not. I guess I know."

John replied, "Who're you kidding? They don't have funerals for live people."

Sue couldn't face John or his disclosure. She ran into the school and blurted out her story to the teacher. The teacher wisely tried to calm Sue, and called her mother on the telephone. When her mother came for Sue, she explained, "Yes, your grandfather died, but we didn't want to tell you. We didn't want to upset you. John should have kept his mouth shut. Now what can I say?"

Sue had no questions she felt she could ask. But she wondered if her grandfather had died because they yelled at him. She wondered why they did not tell her, when Johnny knew. She never thought about her grandfather or about dying without getting an uncomfortable feeling inside. Something had happened to Sue that would take a long time to heal.

Sue couldn't tell her parents that she felt threatened by what had happened, because she could not explain her own feelings. But if she had been able to put them into words, her vague apprehension might have sounded like this: "How could they take Grandpa out and bury him without telling me about it? Didn't they know I loved him? I wonder if they really love me. If I died, would they just take me out and bury me without telling me? Doesn't love mean anything to my father and mother? How can I trust their love if they thought my love for my grandfather didn't mean anything to me?"

It is important for us to realize that the rites and rituals that we use to mark the end of life are our efforts to say a significant and appropriate "good-bye." We don't just dispose quickly of the bodies of those we love as if they were worthless. Some remnants of our love are still attached to them, whether we want to admit it or not. We cannot treat what we have loved without loving care without doing damage to all of the other loving relationships in life. If Sue's parents had understood this, they would have shown more respect for Sue's love, and in return Sue would have had more confidence in the quality of their love for her.

So, the appropriate time to talk about death is when it is part of the child's experience. The proper mood is one of openness and honesty. The important consideration for the adult is that the child's feelings and experiences are quite different from his own and have to be judged accordingly. Then he can share life as far as it can be shared in understanding, and give answers that can be built on as understanding grows. The important relationships that give security to life and love will be protected and nourished then, even in times of emotional stress and painful events.

3. *How to Talk About Death*

IT IS just as important to know how to talk about death as it is to know when to talk about it.

The "how" has to do more with mood and manner than it does with words and methods.

As we pointed out earlier, a child lives largely in a world of feelings, both good and bad. Because he is so dependent upon the adults around him, he is almost defenseless against their feelings. They get to him directly.

The life of the family is built around emotional experiences. When the dealer delivers the new television set, the excitement and joy affects the whole family, and everyone is caught up in the feeling that something new and wonderful has happened. When father drives home in a new car, the whole family "gets into the act" of opening and closing doors, climbing in and out, turning on the car radio and pushing buttons, turning knobs, and in general sharing the joy of getting acquainted with a new possession. When someone in the family is honored by his peers, all the rest join in, as for instance the time when Alvin was elected captain of his Junior League baseball team; all the family went to the playground to watch the games and cheer lustily when Alvin's team was winning and groan appropriately when they were losing.

The life of the family is rooted in the love its members feel for each other. When good things happen, they share them. When painful, disappointing events come along, they are also shared. When Alvin was hit on the bridge of his nose by a pitched ball, both eyes were blackened and swollen nearly shut. The rest of the family took turns reading to him, and, although the black eyes were not fun, all enjoyed the chance to do something special for an ailing member. When the father of Connie's best friend died, all of the family showed their concern by talking about the event, and just being able to talk to someone about it made Connie feel better deep down inside. This love that a family feels for its members is shown in a variety of ways, and the words that express insight and understanding are surrounded by the acts and attitudes that communicate it in many other ways. Patience, understanding, just being near when we need someone near, and a willingness to explain things, tell a child that he is accepted, valued, and loved.

Deep and genuine emotions cannot be denied, for they have their own right to exist. They cannot be locked up in a closet as if they had no right to be there. Even the most uncomfortable feelings need to be faced openly. Usually the feelings of grief are honest and honorable expressions of dismay, disappointment, and pain at the loss of a person who was valued and loved. These feelings cannot be ignored, or told to go away. Where love exists, there is also the possibility of personal distress when the object of love moves away, dies, or is subject to some other major change of status. We cannot act as if these strong feelings did not exist, for to do so would threaten the positive and good feelings that are a part of love and life. We cannot deceive children about our important feelings, for they easily see through our falseness.

We need to be honest with our own deepest feelings. Then it is easier to be honest with the child's. When death comes, our deep feelings cannot be locked up. They are a living part of ourselves, and they are bound to show in our actions and our attitudes. To be able to share these feelings with a child in a way he can accept and understand is important and useful for him, and far more convincing than the effort to deceive him about our feelings and their cause. A child looks to the adults about him for his security in life, and he does not usually see the adults in his world overcome by sadness and the display of strong feelings. The problem then is how to be honest with our own feelings and at the same time be able to continue giving security to the child.

To try to exclude your child from your strong feelings does not work, because he is quick to sense any change in the emotional climate. To be frank and honest about your feelings makes it possible for your child to feel a part of the emotional life of the family, and he feels safer being included than being excluded.

When your child asks, "Why are you crying?" it is far more reasonable to say, "I am sad because your grandmother has died and she won't be around any more. I loved her very much and we will all miss her so," than to say, "Stop asking questions and run along. It is nothing that concerns you and you are too young to understand, anyway." He can handle an honest answer more easily than he can a dishonest evasion.

There is a contagion in strong feeling; to show it is not an act of weakness. Strong feeling may be the evidence of true inner strength. At the very point where the adult may feel threatened by his emotions, the child may feel a type of relationship that he has not known before. Your child, living as he does in a world of emotions, may feel closer to you when your emotions are near the surface than at any other time.

Having said this, however, it is important to realize that the adult has an obligation to temper the expression of his feeling by the wisdom and judgment that characterize maturity. When the adult talks to the child about death, he should remember that sadness is quite different from despair, and that reasonable expression is different from complete collapse. The child should be spared these extreme evidences of adult breakdown, for they would tax his emotional reactions to the breaking point. If your strong emotions get out of hand, your child should not be subjected to them, but should have his communication with you after you have collected yourself and can share your strength rather than your weakness.

When you are overcome by emotion, it takes a special effort to be sensitive to the feelings of a child. The subtle evasions designed to shield your child from emotions you think he could not tolerate are apt to produce the very emotions that he cannot cope with. To be lied to at the same time that he is faced with an emotional climate he cannot understand is doubly injuring. Even half-truths are hard to interpret to a youngster.

The effort to explain death as an event that happens to older persons baffles a child, because time is a new and mysterious idea to him.

When Gary's grandfather, in his sixties, died of a heart ailment, Gary was told that this happened to older persons and he need not be afraid. But Gary felt the emotion in the air, and with a six year old's directness went to work to clarify his understanding. He went first to his eighty-three-year-old great grandmother and said, "Why didn't you die? You're old." Then he went to his grandmother and said, "You're not old, are you?" He asked his father, "How old are you? When will you die?" By the time he got to his mother, she sensed his feeling, and snuggling him beside her she said, "Gary, Gary, don't be frightened. We will probably be with you for a long time. You will grow to be a big man and have little boys and girls all your own, and we'll still be here. You won't be left alone, so don't worry." The combination of death and time and strong feelings all at once made Gary a frightened boy, but his mother's calm reassurance helped to put things right. Yet Gary's mother was not satisfied with her answer, because she knew there would be other times when it would not fit.

It is more difficult to give an explanation of tragic and untimely death. Gary had needed assurance, and she had given it to him. But she thought of other circumstances that would make an expanded answer necessary. She tried to think of what she would say, and an opportunity came like this:

One day when Gary went into the kitchen, she was baking a cake. He waited while she iced the cake and asked for a piece. She explained the cake was not for him but that he could have one of the cupcakes that were still in the oven.

"Who is this for?" Gary asked.

"It's for the Martin family," she explained.

"Why is it for them?" he asked.

"They've had some trouble," she said.

"What kind of trouble?" he queried.

"Mr. Martin was killed in an accident." she answered.

"Oh," said Gary, and asked about his cupcake.

Gary wandered out of the kitchen and made no further comment until later in the day, when he asked bluntly, "Was Mr. Martin old enough to get killed?"

"No, he wasn't. He was too young to die," she replied.

"Then why did he die?" he persisted.

"Sometimes things happen to people that keep them from growing old. Accidents happen, wars happen, or

people get very sick. When that happens, they sometimes die before they are old." She watched to see how
he was taking the answer.

"Did he want to die?" he asked.

"No, I'm sure he didn't. That's why it is important
to be careful so that accidents don't happen. And
that's why we have doctors to get people well." Gary
accepted the answer, and nothing further was said.
But an echo of his thinking showed up several weeks
later when his father was going out in the car. Gary
waved and said, "Goodbye, and don't let any accident
happen to you."

If there is ever a time when complete honesty is
imperative, it is when a child faces an emotional crisis.
Anything that affects the family circle affects him.
This fact is the basic consideration in talking about
death and its meaning. To deceive him then is inex-
cusable. His limited experience is protection against
emotional stress as far as the full meaning of events is
concerned. But dishonesty creates the hazard that
threatens his relations with the adults he depends
on.

This, then, is of primary importance. Share feelings
at the child's level of understanding and at the same
time protect him from the full impact of emotional
breakdown among the adults he depends on for emotional security. He can understand sadness better than
deception. He can build his approach to the future
better on trust than on a lie.

4. *What to Say About Death*

WE FEEL more comfortable with a mystery when we can give a description of what takes place. Death is part of the mystery that surrounds life. Birth is a mystery, and though we can describe the process, adequate explanation is not possible. So with life the precarious balance of heat and cold, light and dark, the oxygen in the atmosphere and the nutrition that sustains life are all mysteries we penetrate in part by our ability to describe what we cannot fully explain. We gain some power over death, at the intellectual level at least, when we understand something of what it is.

The content of our conversations about death will be modified by the age of the child with whom we talk, but what we say will be determined in part by how we are able to describe the process.

With a very young child all that we can do is to point out the difference between life and death, as was suggested by the incident of the dead bird.

With an older child we can point out that death is a

part of the natural order of things. All that is living is also in the process of dying. It may take millions of years for radium to lose its life and become lead, thousands of years for a giant sequoia to live out its life span, or but a few hours for a moth to emerge from its cocoon, lay its eggs, and die. Man lives his three score years and ten, and even if he should live four score, his strength is always engaged in the process of dying. Nothing that lives escapes the natural process of running down or wearing out.

Often the things we take for granted are reminders of the process. Every town has its cemetery. Children play games in them, or even while riding past them. On a long drive our children invented a game that kept them interested for many miles. They counted cemeteries, each on his side of the road, and the one who had counted the most cemeteries by the time we arrived at our destination was the winner. During the long stretches between cemeteries the youngsters raised questions like; "Where did they get all of the people to bury in such a big cemetery in such a little town? or more simply, "Why do they bury people?" This led quite naturally to talk about death and dying that was candid and unemotional, but sound and factual.

As death is natural, it can be described in natural terms. Some death results from organic failure. Death does not happen all at once. Deterioration may take a long time, and the same processes that cause chemical change in the muscles of an athlete who has a charley horse are at work to produce the more extensive chemical change we call *rigor mortis*. Changes in nerve cells of aged persons affect the way they live and think and feel. While the organism may continue to function, some of its parts may be obviously dying. So death is not so far from any of us or so completely a mystery as we at first assume.

But it is not so much what death is that concerns us; rather, it is how we feel about it. For death is not only a natural process. It also has social significance. We become persons through the multiple relationships that make up our lives. We have special feelings for the other persons we share life with. The milkman is important to us in a limited way. A casual acquaintance is different from a close friend because of the quality of the emotions that bind us. We may feel we know the familiar bus driver, though we say no more than a casual "Hello" to him, but our close neighbor has shared many joys and sorrows with us. Death always represents a social loss, but when one close to us dies it tears apart some of the fabric of life, and we have to repair the damage in order to go on.

When death comes to one close to us, deep feelings are let loose because our lives are disrupted. This was the person we talked things over with, and now we can't. This was the person we ate with, played with, traveled with, and now things are changed. We have to learn how to live without the familiar face, the familiar voice, and the familiar ways of doing things. Our ways of living together have to be changed to face the cruel facts of living apart. Sometimes we feel so deprived that life hardly seems worth the trouble. We feel lonely and lost, as if part of our being had been amputated. It may take a while for the deep feelings to be withdrawn from the familiar patterns of life. It may be difficult to do anything without thinking of the person who has died. But gradually the momentum of life forces us to invest more and more of ourselves in the present and the future, and less and less of ourselves in the memories of the past.

Part of our dismay may come from our feeling that if we had a chance to do things over again we would have said and done some things differently. Always when people are close together there is a delicate balance of privilege and responsibility, burden and blessing. Sometimes the burdens and responsibilities seem heavier than they should be, and we say and do things that show our stress and irritation. But usually these things are temporary and we forget them. But when death comes with its awful finality, we tend to go back in our minds and recall the things that we would like to change if we had another chance. But we have to realize that this cannot be done. The record stands, and we have to trust that the person who has died is just as understanding in death as he was in life, when he was quick to understand and forget. Yet we cannot ignore that we have these feelings. We need to face the feelings openly and honestly and try to make the rest of life better for the insight we have gained through the sad experience of death.

Death tests our basic philosophy of life. The things we say about life are bound up with the things we feel about it. This is never more forcefully true than when we face death and try to interpret its meaning.

It is important, then, in speaking to children about death, to make it clear that our grief is not so much for the one who has died as it is a feeling of injury within ourselves. We suffer because we have lost a relationship that we valued, for it sustained our life. Thus the feelings are related to the person who has a chance to readjust to circumstance rather than the person who has died and cannot change what has happened to him.

When we can interpret the social meaning of grief, we create the basis for explaining why we express our grief as we do. We cry because it is a safety valve for our feelings. We try to wash out of our lives the painful and disturbing feelings that exist. It may be hard to explain why crying helps, but from earliest childhood it has been one of the ways we use to show disappointment and to relieve the hurts that develop deep inside of us.

Children are apt to be startled at first when they see an adult cry. It may shatter their idea of adult superiority. It may be because it is often the adult who reprimands them for their tearful moments.

I well remember the impact of parental tears upon my life. It happened when I was eight years old and my sister was six. She died quite unexpectedly of a short-term virus pneumonia, and I was aware of the emotional crisis it caused. My father cried as he paced the floor, repeating out loud, "Oh, if only I had called the doctor sooner." My mother said nothing as she sat quietly sobbing. I had always pictured my father as the completely competent individual, able to wisely manage any situation. Now he was not only crying but also admitting his responsibility for the events that led to my sister's dying. I could not understand all that was involved in dying, but the emotional impact of the collapse of my father's omnipotence was bound up with my feelings of insecurity as well as with my sister's death. I remember feeling very angry at my father for what he said and did, but probably my anger was more closely related to the loss of my father as a security figure in life than it was to the death of my sister, for that I did not fully comprehend.

A wise understanding of the importance of tears and the feelings that go with them can start early in life. A child can be led to feel comfortable with uncomfortable feelings, for strong feelings are not a sign of weakness. To punish a child for crying is to reject his feelings in a way that is doubly injuring to him. It rejects his feelings and it also denies him the chance to be comfortable with the feelings of others when they want to express them vigorously. Perhaps that is why so many persons are strangely uncomfortable in the presence of others who are crying. Young children are often scolded for crying, or at least urged to stop crying, by adults who are made uncomfortable by the feelings expressed. When the child grows older, he is urged to deny his emotions by becoming a good scout, for good scouts never cry. Yet feelings exist, and strong feelings must be expressed, and it is unwise to limit the healthful ways by which this can be done by making it seem improper to use nature's safety valves.

Mrs. Emmett's tears served a doubly useful purpose when the following encounter developed. She was feeling sad because of the death of her college roommate, a close friend through the years. When she received the letter with the sad news, she was alone in the house. She went to her room, closed the door, and was sobbing back through years of memories when the door burst open and five-year-old Arthur entered.

"Mommie, you're crying," he said. "Mommie, why are you crying?"

"I feel sad and I hurt inside," she answered.

"Why do you hurt?" he asked.

"This letter brought me bad news. I had a friend and now the friend is gone," she said.

"Where did your friend go?" he asked.

"She died," was her answer.

"I won't let that bad letter hurt you." Arthur reached for the letter but when his mother laid it on the table and reached for him, he hugged her and said to her what she had often said to him: "I'll kiss you. that will fix it all better again." And he hurried out as abruptly as he had come into the room.

The tears had not been denied or hidden. They were given a reasonable explanation. They were treated as a natural and normal expression of feeling, and the event was over.

When we see someone else cry, we may share their emotions but we can also be glad that they are able to find a safe and healthy release for pent-up feelings. When a child sees an adult crying, the child can understand that he has been hurt and that after a while he will stop crying and feel better.

Death is something that happens to everything that lives, and in time it will happen to everyone who is alive now. But death itself does not hurt, and the person who has died is beyond all physical pain. The pain that is felt is the pain of loss among those who are still alive and able to feel.

Sometimes a simple explanation of the meaning of death to those who have died helps a child to separate his feelings of apprehension about the process of dying from the feelings of those who are lonely and bereaved. Those who feel sadness have the inner power to overcome their feelings with time and go on about their living. So explaining some of the mystery helps to remove it and frees the child to deal wisely with the realities of his experience.

While we are thinking about what to say about death, it is also wise to think of some of the things not to say. Without realizing it, we can implant deep fears of death and unconsciously create a mood of guilt concerning it. How often has a mother looked at the mess her child has made and in mild despair said, "You'll be the death of me." While she did not mean exactly what she said, she did make a connection in the child's mind between his behavior and the death of one he needed and depended on. This could lead to a major guilt problem if something did happen to his mother.

In a family squabble a mother said to her husband in the presence of their two children, "Oh, drop dead, will you." During the next night the husband died of a heart attack. One of the difficult tasks for the mother and the pastor was to try to clarify the nature of the relationship that had existed between husband and wife, so that these last words would not be taken at face value. It is tragic indeed when references to death are so unwise that they create a complicated emotional problem, when death itself is a serious enough fact of life to contend with.

Also, to teach a child to approach sleep each night with a prayer that says, "If I should die before I wake," creates an anxiety that the child is not prepared to handle. To tell a child that death is like going to sleep may complicate his feelings when he is told, "Come now, it is time for you to go to sleep."

Perhaps worst of all is to face some tragic circumstance and tell a child it is God's will. This can shatter his trust at the point where he needs security most, for if God is like a careless criminal or a ruthless and destructive being, it is difficult to believe in his goodness and wisdom. So the child is confused and has received a severe blow at the very center of his capacity for believing. The Scriptures tell us that is it not

God's will that one of his creatures should suffer. Man learns to accept responsibility for his behavior and his violations of God's will when he realizes that the destructive things of life are the denial of God's will, not the expression of it.

5. *How to Say It to Different Ages*

EACH child is an individual. That means that he is unique. There is no one else quite like him. That also means that when things happen to him, he says and does things that are expressions of his uniqueness, and they have to be faced as his way of meeting something new in his life. Children mature at different rates. Growing up is not something that is done by the calendar or a slide rule. It is an individual experience. When important events occur, the child reacts to them in his own unique way. He may act uninterested and unconcerned. He may seem to be overwhelmed by events. Whatever his attitude, it is his own way of expressing himself and his feelings. When a crisis like death comes along in life, the interpretation of it has to be geared to the special characteristics of the child. If he shows little interest, he can be quietly reassured with the realization that his lack of interest may be his way of saying, "I don't want to look at what I see." If, on the other hand, he is endlessly curious, his questions are the frontier of a new and important exploration he is making, and the vigor and persistence with which he does the exploring shows the importance of the subject to him. With this in mind, we can look more closely at the interest and ways of responding that most often characterize different age groups.

A child two or three years of age has little comprehension of the meaning of death. The child lives in the present and has little understanding of time. His life is largely made up of his feelings and his immediate actions. When an emotional experience involving his family relationships occurs, there is little value in or possibility for explanation. What is needed is warmth and reassurance in simple and direct form. This may be done by holding the child in your arms and talking calmly to him about the things he knows. It is important to be able to share as much of his life with him as possible in the ways he has experienced it in the past. Time and distance and the structure of relationships important to the older child are not yet a part of his experience, but tender love and care are.

The young child is aware of emotional changes. When he pesters you to "Tell me a story" or "Play with me," he is asking for assurance that in the midst of changed feelings and actions he can be sure that things are the same for him. During times of family emotional crisis he is sustained by large doses of warmth and love and interest in him and the world as he knows it.

When the child reaches the early school years, his world has grown. He knows more people and he has a

new feeling for time and distance. Yesterday and to-
morrow have more meaning, but the meaning of death
is still too large an idea to grasp easily. So he takes
hold of it where he can. He may be able to understand
that his grandfather will not be able to come and visit
him any more, but the finality of death still may be out
of his reach. He will show this by asking questions like,
"Is Granddaddy still in the hospital?" He can understand something of the nature of death by simple
analogy. You can tell him, "Granddaddy became old
and his body did not suit him any more so he moved
out of it. His body had aches and pains and he was
uncomfortable in it. Granddaddy still exists but he
doesn't live in his body any more." Such an idea gives
room for growth in his thinking about death, does not
deny the reality of the physical event, and fits his
capacity for adjusting to the physical absence of a person who has been a familiar part of his world.

By the time a child is eight or nine years old, he has
probably traveled far enough to have expanded his
horizons. He has studied other countries and their
peoples. His capacity for grasping enlarged ideas has
developed. However, large ideas still have their focus
upon himself, his life, and his feelings. When the father of a nine-year-old boy died, the child's grief was
centered about an unfinished racing car he and his
father were making. His disappointment was real
enough, but it was related to the point at which he and
his father were sharing life. At this age many children
have had enough religious training to have some idea

of a soul. Though the concept is not formed in spiritual terms, there is a growing awareness of life's mysteries, and the mystery of death can be related to the other mysteries of life. Here the relation of personality to the physical equipment of life has meaning. The separation of body and spirit can be understood in functional terms: If the pianist had left the piano, the familiar music would not be heard, for the two must go together.

When a child is eleven or twelve, his mind is beginning to furnish abstractions with meanings that have significance for him. Love is an emotion he feels in new ways. He can enter into the feelings of others and understand more of what the loss incurred by death means. He is able to talk about his feelings not merely in terms of himself but with an understanding of how others feel. He has some idea of energy and the scientific insight into the relation of energy and matter. He understands that when coal is burned there is smoke, ash, and energy. He can also understand that death involves changes that may release spiritual energy in the form of a soul that functions apart from the body. While the ideas are still far from explicit, he takes his science and his religion and his growing understanding of relationships and gets a more mature idea of what death means physically and spiritually. His sensitivity for the feelings of others makes it possible for him to share their grief with understanding and a desire to be helpful. This desire can be used to help him resolve his own feelings of loss.

The adolescent is apt to mix his own emotional problems with the crises that come to his life. It is difficult to separate the emotions that are directly related to the situation from those which are triggered by it to release deeper problems that have been lurking unseen. The stories of two adolescents will show how these problems merge as they develop.

Edward J. was fourteen, sensitive and shy. He was having a difficult time making friends in the community to which his family had recently moved. A puppy, Lassie, was more than ordinarily important to him, for she gave him the affection he needed. When he was not in school they were constantly together, and at night she curled up at the foot of his bed. Because the family home was on a heavily traveled highway, Edward was impressed with his responsibility for making sure that Lassie was always properly secured. One day Edward crossed the street and neglected to tie up the puppy. She tried to follow him, but was hit by a car, and so seriously injured that the veterinarian felt obliged to give her a lethal injection to relieve her of the misery of a hopelessly injured spine.

This produced an emotional crisis for Edward. He did not want to face his guilt, so he blamed the driver of the car and the veterinarian for what had happened. He made threatening statements concerning them, and spent hours pacing back and forth in his room. His parents tried to talk with him, but he said, "Nobody can say anything to bring Lassie back, so keep still." Efforts to divert his attention were useless. He would

not consider getting another dog because he thought
that would be unfaithful. He became increasingly difficult to guide or understand, and on advice of the
school psychologist was taken to a child guidance center. Here it was established through testing that an
unusually large amount of anxiety had been centered
about the death of the pet. He could not bear to face
the full impact of his guilt and so was retreating into a
state of emotional illness. Skilled treatment was necessary in order to help him face the reality of what had
happened, accept his failure and learn from it, and
then get on with the important tasks of living.

The grief event often releases feelings that have not
been observed, and the child may suffer from emotional reactions too strong to handle by himself. Then
it is that wise parents and a sensitive society come to
his aid.

Marian was fifteen, and proud of her brother who
was in the Navy. It was during wartime, communica-
tions were limited, but she knew her brother was on
a ship in the Pacific. A telegram came to her parents
saying that her brother was "missing in action and
presumed lost." Personal events in Marian's life gave
special meaning to this tragic news. The preacher in
her church often spoke of sex activity as sinful, and
warned of inevitable punishment to come from it. He
belabored the point that sex sins caused tragic consequences for all who engaged in them. Marian had par-
ticipated in some mild expressions of affection on a
date shortly before the telegram arrived. In her mind

there was no doubt that the behavior which she had been led to believe was sinful had caused the death of her brother.

Overlooking the fact that the war might have been the cause, Marian accepted an overwhelming burden of guilt. She dared tell no one of her feelings because she felt it was bad enough to know what had happened without adding the judgments of others. She became withdrawn and depressed. Friends said, "She's taking her brother's death very hard." She did not have anything to do with boys for a long time, and when she did accept an occasional date, she was cold and reserved. When she finally married, she showed her burden of guilt through an unhappy sex relationship, and only when it brought the marriage close to the breaking point did a wise counselor get to the root of Marian's emotional problem. With patience and understanding she was helped to work through it.

One does not easily know what goes on in the mind of an adolescent, but any deep emotional crisis invites a special effort to be aware of unusual behavior, so that help can be made available before many years of suffering and anguish of spirit are endured.

The fifteen- or sixteen-year-old has a stage of mental development where abstractions are often more important than the world of outer reality. He reaches for meanings and values and philosophizes at great length. Though he may not talk freely with his parents, he spends many hours talking with friends and other adults about the feelings, experiences, and ideas that come to him. Although his emotions seem unstable, he is rapidly moving toward adult ways of thinking. For him the spiritual interpretation of death comes quite naturally, and he can assume the attitude and role of an adult in considering such matters. He is able to assume responsibility and wants to prove his competence. In many instances his capacity for abstract thinking leads him toward religious participation. He thinks of himself as an adult and wants others to think of him that way.

Although age-group classifications may be helpful in understanding the general characteristics of a child, it is always wise to keep in mind that each child is an individual shaped by the experience of his life. The studies by A. L. Gesell help to define the intellectual and emotional nature as well as the behavior of children of different ages, but as each child is an individual, so each child must be given a chance to express his feelings in his own way.

This makes it important for adults to be sensitive and responsive to the moods and attitudes of children and youth, so that they may have a clearer picture of just what is happening in their emotional and social being. When this is done, these young personalities can be helped to face the crises of life caused by death, so that they will grow through them to become more competent persons.

It is well to remember that the adult emotions surrounding death are compounded from the growth process and always include feelings of deprivation, biological questions, and social ramifications as well as psychological, spiritual, and religious responses. A child from birth to three or four can sense loss but cannot conceptualize death. His feelings invite love, reassurance, and emotional support. From four through seven, biological interests will take the center of the stage and will have to be met with simple, direct biological answers. From eight through twelve the meaning of death will acquire a social dimension, and the concern for the consequences of death on the lives of the living will be paramount. From thirteen through the years of adolescence the main effort will be to seek a psychological, spiritual, or religious meaning for death, which is a part of the teen-age quest for the meaning in life. Every normal grief experience will have these elements, for the growth of the emotion is cumulative. The adult needs to have reassurance, a chance to face the biological meaning of death, an encounter with its social meaning, and a satisfaction of his needs to fit it into a psychological and religious pattern. When any phase of the developmental process is mishandled, it will tend to complicate the adult response.

6. *Why Talking It Over Is Important*

WE HAVE learned much in recent years about the importance of talking through a problem as a way toward solving it. The right words said at the right time have a healing value. This is especially true of the emotions, though it is also true of mental and physical states, for there is no part of life where the feelings are not bound up with thinking and with those physical conditions that are related to good health.

Many of the conditions that surround the mystery of death can be relieved by giving information that dispels the unknown. A child is usually actively interested in the physical circumstances concerning death and what is done to the bodies of dead persons. They wonder about what the funeral director does and what takes place at the funeral. They wonder what people do when they go to the funeral home and perhaps stay for hours.

Even for adults these mysterious happenings create feelings of discomfort. The best way to dispel them is to be willing to talk about them freely and honestly. But sometimes the adult does not have the information he needs, so we will supply some of the essential facts here.

The funeral director is a person professionally trained to meet certain legal and health requirements. He has a special place equipped to prepare bodies for burial. This practice has ancient roots, and every civilization has shown its respect for life by burying its dead with ceremony. Often this involves preparing the bodies so that they will delay the chemical processes that set in immediately after death. This is called embalming. The Egyptians did it in early times with rare skill. In the time of Jesus it was done by friends of the family. In early times it was done with spices, herbs, and perfume. Now it is done more scientifically with chemicals.

All of the important events of life are surrounded with appropriate ceremonies. Because a baby is considered valuable, parents show their appreciation for their partnership with God in the creating of the new life by baptism or an act of dedication. When students graduate from school or college, there is stately ceremony. When a community leader is honored, it is done with fitting rites. When a couple marries, the community recognizes the importance of the new home being established by attending the wedding ceremony. When a person who is loved and valued by the community comes to the end of his days, his physical remains are treated with respect, and a fitting ceremony, called a funeral service, recognizes the value of his life and the grief felt at his death. This is one of the marks of civilization, and it is important to the living because by it we preserve and perpetuate the value attached to human personality.

Some of the things that are done at the time of death may not at first be understood by a child. It is important that he should have a chance to find out. Many of the questions a child wants to ask are quite simple and concerned with physical things. One little girl was sent to me with some questions. I wanted to know exactly what it was that concerned her, so I asked her to tell me just what she wanted to know. Her questions were, "Do dead people have their eyes open or closed?" "Are dead people lying down or standing up?" and "Are they dressed or do they have their pajamas on?" These were simple questions to answer, and they dispelled the mystery that lurked in her mind.

Most children wonder about cemeteries and crematories. Again it is important to know exactly what questions are in their minds before answering. If they ask, "Why do they put dead people in the ground?" It is reasonable to point out that everything comes from the ground and returns to it. The food we eat grows in the ground. The fruit trees have their roots in the ground. Cows that give milk graze upon the grass, and we live and play on the earth. All we do is related to the ground, so it is quite proper that when the body no longer is needed it be put back in the ground. It may help the child to know that we take good care of the things we value, and so the body is put in a special kind of container called a casket. The crematory is just another place for disposing of the body that is not needed any more, except that here the process of return of the elements to the earth is done more rapidly. Instead of letting the slow process of disintegration take place, fire is used to do the same thing more quickly. In India, for instance, it has long been the practice to have a ceremonial burning of the body that is no longer needed.

When the events surrounding death are new to the child, his questions may be numerous. The questions he asks are an expression of his feelings, and they need to be dealt with respectfully. When his questions are answered calmly and honestly, he feels more comfortable about what has happened, and much of the fear and dread that existed in his mind are dispelled.

Death will stimulate new and uncomfortable feelings. A child may have considerable curiosity about the new and turbulent emotions around him. The adult who is willing and able to accept his feelings keeps open the door to his questions.

Your child may ask about the funeral service. He may even want to go to it. This is probably unwise for the young child, but children who can sit through a short public service might better be allowed to attend than denied the chance to share in something they know is important to the family. However, no child should be forced to attend against his wishes, for this may injure his feelings in ways that are not apparent. It may be wiser to have the child visit the funeral home with a calm and trusted adult who is willing to share the experience with him and answer his questions with understanding and patience.

Many questions are precipitated by current events and the newspaper headlines. So it was with the questions of eleven-year-old Wendy. She lived much of her free time in a world of illusion created by Hollywood. She absorbed movie magazines in stacks, and lived and thought of handsome men and glamorous women. It was a shock to her when news came that the queen of her world of illusion was dead, not because of physical illness, accident, or old age but because she ended her own life. When she asked her mother for an explanation, she was not satisfied with the first superficial efforts and persisted with the question.

"But what I want to know is why she did it."

Realizing that no superficial answer would be good enough, Wendy's mother said, "When a person takes his own life, I think he is sick, but it is a different kind of sickness. It is an inside sickness—the feelings are ill."

Wendy responded, "I don't get it. She always looked healthy and happy in her pictures. Why was she sick inside?"

Wendy's mother tried again, "Sometimes a person is so disappointed with life that it doesn't seem worth living. He may have material things but misses something he needs deep inside of himself, like love. This makes him depressed. Depression is a kind of sickness. When a person takes his life, he may be suffering from that sickness."

Wendy thought a while and asked, "Does that sickness hurt?"

"Yes, very much," her mother answered. "But it is a hurt you feel deep inside, like sadness."

"Can they do anything to make people better when they have that sickness?" Wendy asked.

"Yes," her mother said. "Many people are sad but not many so sad they cannot endure it. When they get that kind of sickness, they go to a special kind of doctor who treats sick feelings, and usually they get well again."

Wendy meditated again and seemed to close the subject, for the time being at least, with the comment, "It's too bad she didn't have a doctor who could make her well inside. She was so pretty outside."

Many of the emotions that a child experiences can be handled so that anxiety is dispelled and understanding is increased. If he is not able to express his feelings in healthy ways, they may become tangled up in fear, horror, and morbid curiosity that will show itself for years to come.

Fear can be contagious, but so is confidence. What happens to the child when he wants to talk through the questions that come popping into his mind is important. His curiosity and his questions are his way of showing his feelings. This is an opportunity to help prepare him for the crises that are so much a part of

human experience. Everyone faces the death of someone near to him on an average of once every six years
throughout life. The child who develops confidence in
meeting this experience in his early years has a foundation that he can build on for many years to come. It
is a healthy thing to be able to talk out the questions
and get calm and mature answers when they are
needed most.

7. Understanding the Nature and Treatment of Children's Grief

STUDIES of grief show that young, old, and middle-aged people express their grief in different ways. This may mean that you must make an extra effort to understand what is going on in the thoughts and feelings of people in age groups different from your own.

A person in the middle years tends to show his grief through emotional reactions. He is normally in his vigorous years physically and is well organized and competent in meeting the demands of daily life. So it is quite natural that he would show his reaction to crisis at the point at which the emotional stress is most acute.

Older people tend to show their grief through physical symptoms. They suffer aches and pains and may develop some of the diseases that reflect their loss of interest in life. Their eyesight and hearing may become impaired. They may show the symptoms of restricted movement caused by rheumatism and arthritis. It is a time of life when the emotions are less active and the physical organism is beginning to run down, and the weakest parts first show the results of stress and strain.

With children the feelings of grief are more apt to be worked out in their behavior. We noted earlier how in some instances this is shown in juvenile delinquency. Other forms of behavior fall short of this classification but still show that the grief is being worked through in various types of behavior. This is quite natural, for children are active beings and their feelings show through this activity.

Sometimes little children try to comprehend the idea of death by playing dead. They usually do it with other children and say, "Now make believe I'm dead." Whether the game is elaborate, with doctors and ministers and funeral directors, or whether it is simple, it is the effort to deal experimentally with the unknown though role-playing. Sometimes adults are invited to take part in the play and because of their strong feelings may not want to make a game of something so serious. But if it is possible to understand the importance of role-playing for the child, it may be possible to share the activity and by participation add creatively to the understanding of a new and difficult idea.

Sometimes a child will show his grief through anger. He feels deprived of something important in his life, and because he cannot understand what has happened he relates his feelings to the rest of his experience. He may get angry with his toys and break them, and fail to know why he does it. To scold the child for breaking his toys without understanding why he does it or the feelings he is trying to express through it is interpreted by the child as a rejection of his feelings.

Sometimes the connection between the anger and the behavior is clearly seen. At other times it is obscured. Billy was reprimanded repeatedly for playing baseball near a greenhouse, yet he led his friends in playing in a vacant lot near the greenhouse. When he came to bat he was overcome by an urge to hit the ball toward the forbidden building. When he saw the ball sail toward the greenhouse and heard the glass shattering, he knew what would happen, but it seemed to be worth the price. Although he was punished, scolded, and made to pay for the broken glass, no one seemed to feel it was important to find out why he did what he did. Even Billy was not aware of the fact that greenhouses and flowers were associated in his mind with funerals and death, and by his action he was directly assaulting the visible symbols of what had caused him grief. The indirect expressions of anger are no less real because they are devious.

At other times the child may be overcome with a feeling that he is going to be abandoned. If one parent dies he will cling to the other with tenacity. He may not want to go to school because he is afraid that when he comes home he will find himself completely alone. He will try to keep his other parent always in sight, and may actually hold on physically hour after hour. To become impatient with his behavior and try to shake loose from his grip is a further threat. It is important to interpret such behavior for what it is—a type of grief expression—and deal with it patiently and with understanding. It is wise to give repeated assurance by saying, "You can let go now, for I will be right here." Or, "I know how you feel, but don't be afraid for I'll be right nearby." Usually such conditions pass more quickly if accepted and shared. At other times the child may want to do things with the adults in the family. He may want to go where they go, participate in their activities, stay up later to make sure they are still there, and in varied ways show that he feels threatened and in danger of further abandonment. It is reasonable to make concessions to a strict schedule in order to give reassurance in as many ways as possible to the threatened child.

Sometimes a child will substitute other feelings for the ones that are hard to handle. He may become boisterous and noisy, as if to reassure himself by his own noise. He may employ his childish sense of humor to laugh about things that are not really funny. We all have a tendency to joke about the serious things of life as if this brings them down to a size where we can take hold of them. It is quite true that laughing and crying are closer to the same root emotions than we usually think. Sometimes even overt cruelty becomes a grief expression. One lad was caught squeezing baby chicks to death. When scolded and asked why he would do such a thing, he answered candidly, "I wanted to feel what dying was like." He grew up to be a physician, using his hands to save life rather than destroy it. It is important to understand the meanings of the various types of behavior and interpret them wisely, for they, too, work themselves out more quickly if accepted for what they are—grief acted out in behavior.

The strong emotions of grief can be compounded by exclusion. Mildred grew up to be an inveterate gossip. She wanted to know all there was to know about everybody and everything. If she could not find out, she made it up out of imagination, and was always in trouble for spreading stories that were not quite true. When she was a child, she was systematically excluded from "adult talk." She was thoughtlessly sent from the room when certain subjects, like birth and death, were mentioned. She remembers these times as exceedingly painful, and she has been spending the later years of her life by talking about all of the subjects that she was not allowed to hear about when she was a child.

So the child does not want to be excluded. When company comes, he wants to get in the center of the group so he can hear all that is said. The child's problem is a difficult one. He wants to know what is largely beyond his capacity to know, and he wants to understand what is beyond his understanding. If he can be accepted and included in what is going on around him, he will feel that nothing else is going to happen that he cannot at least see and share in.

A child can be helped to meet these states of mind and emotion by those who understand that his personality and his behavior are two parts of the same being. His emotion is deep and baffling and he must express it in the only way that he knows, through his behavior.

Your child is quickly responsive to reassurance. The warm and kindly acceptance of his behavior as an extension of his feeling makes him comfortable. The calm and reassuring words repeated many times in many different ways helps to sustain him. Just to say, "We love you and we are not going off and leave you," makes him feel secure.

Information is helpful, and in talking things over, he should have solid facts to hold on to. This is the material he uses to frame the world of his experience. He is threatened by death because it is unknown and it happens to people and he feels it may happen to him. He needs to know that when one person dies it does not mean that others are also going to die quickly, as if death were a contagious disease. It helps him to know that other people about him expect to live for a long time yet.

Sometimes the reassurance comes through special efforts to be close rather than through words. A child feels complimented when an adult shares his play, and one of the most important invitations in life does not come on an engraved card, but is the simple appeal, "Come play with me."

Because grief is a feeling compounded of uncertainty, loss, insecurity, and fear, it is important to make every effort to give the child information where possible, closeness and warmth in many ways, and the evidence of adult calmness and confidence in order to dispel the fears that facing the unknown often generates.

Yes, your child's grief is real, though it may vary in its forms of expression. To be reassured, loved, and understood is of great importance to your child and will help him grow through the painful experience to be a stronger person in the future experiences of his life.

8. *The Long-Range Values to Be Considered*

As WE look at the things we do to help a child face the adjustments that come with the death of someone close to him, we need to keep certain long-range values in mind.

We need to know that we are helping the child to develop some discriminating values concerning death, for not all death is the same. There is a difference between the death that comes to an aged person at the end of the natural cycle of life and the death that comes with untimely suddenness to a young person through tragic accident. One can be accepted calmly as though long expected, while the other has the elements of accute disappointment and injustice. There is a difference between the illness that takes a person in his best years and the terminal event that marks the wearing out of a well-used organism.

The different attitudes toward different types of death reflect our values. We resist illness and place a high value on health. We show our values by trying to do the things that protect good health and overcome illness. We react to tragic accidents with a feeling that they did not need to be, and so we develop the caution and carefulness that is protection against them. If children learn that death is natural for the aged but unnatural for the young, they have gained a resource for learning caution and valuing health.

Some of the behavior of modern youth is an expression of a morbid curiosity about death that shows inadequate values concerning life. The game called "chicken," where teen-agers race toward each other in their cars to see which one will pull out first and be called chicken, is a form of behavior that is related to this flirting with death out of curiosity. It is the American form of Russian roulette, in which a person gambles with death as a way of showing his inadequate valuation of life. It is the teen-agers' mental way of saying, "See, I am not afraid of death." But it is false, for it shows an unhealthy effort to prove to themselves that they do not fear what in truth is an overwhelming mystery to them. If they make light of it, it might go away, but it never does. Like whistling in the dark, it gives no real security, but only makes the sound that sounds like reassurance. A wise handling of the questions about life and death in the early years makes this reckless folly unreasonable and unnecessary.

Also, a wise and perceptive approach to the problems of early childhood helps to create the values that make healthy adjustment to reality a natural process.

An honest facing of facts is part of the equipment for normal living. This is nowhere more important than in facing the facts of death as a prerequisite for building a mature philosophy of life. A structure of escape and illusion is a futile foundation for emotional security and wise living. A wise teacher centuries ago warned about building life on a foundation of sand. Only the solid rock of fact is an adequate base for the structure of life. Only when the most difficult facts of human experience are met with serenity and sound judgment can the events of life be properly judged and the adjustments of mature thinking and feeling be made.

Through the wise facing of death one can learn to live with his own deep feelings and value the rights of others to have their deep feelings also. More than we realize, the good life grows from the capacity to handle strong emotions wisely and well. When feelings get so completely out of control that they destroy life, we have real tragedy. When strong feelings are accepted and handled within the bounds of sound expression and wise action, we have gone a long way toward learning how to live.

The development of inner resources grows from a realization that the person has within himself the capacities for meeting the incidents of life as if they were incidental. Only then does he keep clearly in mind that life itself is the real value. What sustains it is good, and what destroys it is evil. Upon this foundation mature and healthy religion is built. The capacity to accept one's self and one's feelings and accept others with their moods and attitudes is basic to being able to feel at home in the universe, for it is the expression of the faith that life is not an illusion but is rather the ultimate source of meaning. When one has built a structure of values one understands what is meant by an "abundant life" as well as what is implied by the commandment, "Love God with heart and soul and mind and strength, and thy neighbor as thyself."

The religious foundations of life are more basic than the forms or rituals of any religious organization. A feeling for life may be sustained and enriched by religious activities, but it is always basic to and prior to the forms that are employed. The true religious sense is built into the consciousness of the individual as he grows to value life—his own and the lives of others. An honest facing of death may be one of the points at which this true valuation of life is achieved in the soul of the individual.

Becoming an adult is not only a matter of years or physical maturity. Rather, it is a competence in understanding life. Some people become physically mature but continue to live emotionally in rompers. They cannot face life, with its deprivations and its privileges, without retreating into inappropriate emotional attitudes. Much of this immaturity may be traced to an improper handling of the meaning of life when it was interpreted at time of death.

The emotional capacity of the child usually grows with experience. It is unfortunate if an unwise or emotionally overwrought adult has thrown a road block in the way of the healthy emotional development of a child. Actual experience in withstanding deprivation fortifies life. The false promises, the illusory attitude toward death, and the practices of immature religion are a handicap for life rather than a resource for its living.

The opportunity to help a child face reality and handle his deep emotions wisely is a privilege to be treasured. It invites the care and competence of one who is deeply concerned with both the immediate and the long-term results. When this help is given, the child moves into his future better equipped for life. Though he may not know it or be able to express it adequately, he owes a debt of gratitude to the adults who have wisely furnished him with sound resources for his inner development.

9. *The Adult Helps Himself When He Helps the Child*

IT IS characteristic of our culture that we try to develop intellectual substitutes for our deep emotions. We try to intellectualize and rationalize grief. But our deep feelings have their own validity and ultimately they must be dealt with as feelings. It is never a matter of choosing whether or not emotions will be expressed but rather of deciding whether or not they will be expressed wisely. Medical studies reveal that certain illnesses appear to be the results of repressed and suppressed emotion. When the feelings cannot find a normal and healthy expression, they are diverted and show up later in physical symptoms.

This is often the case with the emotions that are attendant upon grief. Because we are taught that it is important to be brave, we think this means that we should deny our feelings the right they have to be expressed in appropriate form. So we develop intellectual devices as substitutes for expressing our feelings, and this is neither wise nor effective.

We need to know that the things done at the time of death have the primary purpose of helping us give vent to our feelings. The funeral is not primarily for the dead but for the living. It gives a traditional and approved setting within which strong feelings can be expressed and accepted by the community as proper and appropriate. In fact, it becomes a time when the community helps to create the atmosphere in which deep feelings can be brought to the surface and expressed.

When the adult who is inclined to deny his feelings comes face to face with a child who is not afraid to let his feelings go, a healthy interchange may take place. I have talked with adults who said that what did them the most good was trying to be helpful to a child who was asking direct and sometimes embarrassing questions. The adult was then obliged to face squarely the things he was trying to avoid, and in doing so he found the healthy emotional release that he needed.

The emotions are rooted in lower levels of consciousness, in what we call the unconscious and the subconscious. This is the storehouse of repressed or suppressed thought and feeling. The meanings that we consciously deal with may be well within the range of intellectual activity and yet leave the deeper level of emotions unsatisfied. This is illustrated by the effect of words that have many levels of meaning. For instance, the family is sitting in the waiting room of the hospital anxiously waiting for a report from the doctor who is attending the dying patient. Finally the physician comes into the waiting room and says to the family,

"It's all over. I'm sorry to have to tell you that your loved one is dead." Everyone who is listening knows what the word "dead" means intellectually. All of them believe the doctor. All of them hear adequately. They know the meaning, and yet some part of the being is not yet convinced. Some level of being does not grasp the full implications of the word. It rebels against the meaning and tries to protect itself from the pain of full realization. This part of the being wants to deny the fact, and it is this part that has to be convinced before a healthy readjustment to life can begin.

Until the deeper level of the emotions is convinced, the true work of mourning cannot begin and the adjustment to the new circumstances of life cannot properly proceed. An acute physical pain may make a person faint. This is a way nature uses to blot out an intolerable physical pain. The same thing is true when an intolerable emotional pain is felt. The person may try to deny the painful fact. He may use various devices to do this. He may take sedation or alcohol to blot out his feelings. He may use intellectual sedation to deny the full consciousness of what has happened. But these escapes from reality are never good enough to build a life on or face the future with.

In his effort to answer the questions of a child, the troubled adult may find that he is not only answering his own questions but is beginning to face his own feelings honestly. When he interprets the natural course of life with its inevitable event of death, he moves himself beyond the immediate event to a larger context within which it fits. When he tries to explain why a person feels so badly when one he loves dies, he opens up the channels through which his own deeper feelings may find an outlet. In fact, in being honest with a child he learns how to be honest with himself and with the feelings that stir the depths of his being.

At the same time that he serves his own needs for reassurance and honest acceptance of feeling, he is also doing something else that is important for him as well as for his child. He discovers that there are channels of communication concerning thought and feeling where he is still part-child himself. At this point he can enter into the world of the child and find a new tolerance for his feelings at the same time that he is helping the child to grow toward a more adult way of looking at life and its varied events. At this point the gap between the generations is bridged and the most fruitful communication grows. It may well be that this becomes the major turning point in the relationship between the adult and child, for at the point at which deep feelings exist they are truly close to each other and become aware in new ways of the need they have for each other.

Life is never a simple or uncomplicated process. New occasions teach new duties. Growth is not an even process, for sometimes a person grows up a lot in a short time. The emotional crises are times when rapid growth toward a wise handling of experience can take place. The task of telling a child about death may grant privileged moments to the adult who understands the importance of the process for the child. At the same time, he may find that he himself has a chance to do some rapid growing as he concludes some of the unfinished business of his own childhood.

10. *Telling the Child About Death*

WE HAVE looked at the impact of death on the life and experience of the child from a number of angles. Now it seems important to point out why it is doubly important for us to give special consideration to the whole subject in our culture. Our experience of death is different from that of any other era in history. The effective separation of death from life is one of the by-products of specialization.

A hundred years ago death, like birth, growth, and the other events in life, was home-centered. People lived close to it, and though it might be painful it was a clean, uninfected wound. It was natural, not remote. It was a part of life and not an unapproachable mystery. Now the situation has changed markedly. Nearly all dying is done away from the home, in hospitals in the presence of professional persons, doctors and nurses. Even the aging process is removed from the home, and the segregation of senior citizens in colonies for retired persons tends to give the normal life cycle a contorted look.

The effect of all this is that something unreal is introduced into the context of living. When an important part of life is removed from normal experience, it tends to be anxiety-creating. When, during the Victorian era, birth, sex, and puberty were removed from common conversation, a vacuum of interest was created and anxiety moved in. It took a couple of generations to correct the problem, and even now remnants of the anxiety persist.

In our day the experience of death has been removed not only from the normal context of home life but also from the conversation of many people. Now sophisticated parents, who talk easily with their children about sex and birth, find it hard to speak with them about death and its meaning. But when anything as prevalent as death is excluded from easy communication, it creates an emotional vacuum into which fear and anxiety, mystery and uncertainty come.

When something like this happens in the life of a culture, deliberate and careful action is needed to correct it. We must realize the importance of ways of talking about death, and ways of doing things at the time of death, for the prevention of anxiety and the proper framing of reality in the total experience of both children and adults. Because many adults have unwittingly become a part of the conspiracy of silence and unreality concerning death, it is doubly important for them to understand how they can contribute to the correcting of an unhealthy social and emotional state.

Some of this can be done by a deliberate effort to

talk through important emotional events in family life so that anxiety can be drained from them. Such events do not always have to mention death. Leonard overheard his mother talking about a certain physician who had served the family for many years. In the presence of a serious illness she had some doubts about the doctor's competence and suggested that another physician, a specialist, be consulted. In the presence of the child she made disparaging remarks about the doctor and his basic intelligence and repeated some trivial gossip she had heard about him and his personal habits. Evidently the adults in the family thought little about the matter, and a month or so later the critical situation had corrected itself. But the lingering doubts planted in the mind of young Leonard persisted. They become acute when he fell ill and the family doctor was summoned. Leonard was afraid of him, questioned his mother's love because she had called a physician she did not trust, and decided she didn't really care what happened to him. The anxiety let loose in the child's life because he had grasped only part of the meaning of an important event in family life produced an agonizing crisis for Leonard. It would have been prevented if careful thought had been given to what was said, or if once having been said, it could have been talked about openly so that Leonard's doubts and fears could have been resolved. How often adults unwittingly destroy the faith of children in the persons who bring professional skills to the service of their communities by idle and unprofitable talk.

Sometimes the child's fear is attached to the hospital just because of things he hears said about people being rushed to the hospital in an ambulance, or not getting there in time. Instead of thinking of the medical center as a blessing to the community and its people, the child may well be conditioned to think of it with fear and apprehension. If and when he is obliged to go to the hospital, he is filled with doubts and painful thoughts.

Often parents say things to children in the effort to control behavior that the child interprets in a different way. It has almost become a routine in Jane's home for her mother to say, "If you don't want to be sick, take your vitamins." Jane developed a persistent low-grade fever that slowly sapped her strength, and the doctors decided she should go to the hospital for tests. When her parents went to visit Jane, they found she was irritable and surly and acted as if she did not want to talk with them. The nurses, however, said that she was an ideal patient, cooperative and cheerful. Jane's parents were baffled by her behavior, but because they had developed the practice of talking out even the unpleasant events of life, they asked Jane about her actions toward them. Jane blurted out that it was their fault that she was there. She had recalled the daily threat about the vitamins and decided that since she had missed them a few times her parents had willed her illness as a punishment. Naturally Jane resented this, but when it was talked about her parents were able to correct her impression, and then the irritability and anger disappeared.

Distressing events can be useful if they can be discussed with a clear concern for the child's thoughts and feelings. Even events surrounding death can be used creatively if it is recognized that it is important to do so.

The wise use of the educational opportunity that comes with death is illustrated in the dilemma of a mother with five children, whose oldest died as a result of a shooting accident. She wanted to be able to talk about the tragic event with the younger children naturally and normally, but was concerned that the restoration of the body would make this impossible. She talked with the funeral director about her concern, and he suggested that he place a bandage around the head at the place of the wound. This was done, and made it easier to talk about the event realistically and constructively. Wise funeral practice should help to confirm reality rather than deny it. This is a sound educational premise in dealing with experience.

Quite an unwise procedure was used by the parents of Tony and Bob. Their sister was ill of leukemia in a nearby hospital. No mention was ever made of the illness to the brothers. On Christmas day great preparations were made for a visit of a few hours when the sick girl was released from the hospital for a brief time. Two weeks after Christmas she died, and again no explanation of any kind was made to the boys. Their anxious questions were turned aside. The family stoically went through the rituals of their church but did not include the boys. The subject of their sister and what had happened to her was a closed matter.

Tony and Bob felt very much threatened by the whole matter. They wanted to talk about it and what it meant for them. Could they die without anyone saying anything about it? Did their parents really love them? The boys showed their feelings of insecurity in different ways. Tony, who was twelve, began taking things that didn't belong to him. When he was caught, his parents punished him severely and said, "What shall we have to endure next?" Bob, who had done well in school in the past, now became listless and preoccupied, and as a result brought home a report card with failing marks. He was punished and his parents declared that there was no end to the suffering their children were inflicting on them. So, as the adults continued to react to their grief irrationally, their children were caught up in the tragic circumstances. It was only when school authorities, who sensed the deeper meaning of their behavior, referred the problem to a child guidance center that the parents began to work through their feelings and, at the same time, develop new understanding of the actions of Tony and Bob.

In a death-denying, death-defying culture, it is more important than ever before to develop wise and healthful ways of facing reality and talking through its emotional impact. Hospitals for the mentally ill list as high as 9 per cent of their newly admitted patients as suffering from acute grief reactions. Studies of certain types of mental illness show that the roots of the anxiety are often found in the unresolved grief of adults who have passed on their anxiety to their children.

Dr. James A. Knight says that the major field of psychosomatic research today is the organic behavior that is the physical expression of the anxiety felt by those who suffer death, separation, and loss.

The whole problem of a wise approach to death in our culture is not a trivial matter. It may well be one of the major emotional concerns of our time. If we can develop wise and healthful ways of coping with it, we can reduce the size and importance of the problem. If we cannot learn to do that, it will undoubtedly become a problem of ever-increasing proportions.

This is no judgment from an ivory tower. I am deeply serious about this matter. I have seen the powerful impact upon life of unwisely handled death experiences. I have seen it in children in a clinic. I have seen it in adults in hospitals where neuroses and psychoses have been the end result of intolerable anxiety. I have seen people who have lost their will to live because they were so overwhelmed by fear of death. I have seen people become impotent in the face of important life crises because their anxiety possessed them so completely that their fear of death made them afraid to live.

Perhaps when the history of this era is written it will be pointed out that this was the age of great anxiety, when the inability of people to face life and death produced a crippling philosophy of life. Wise in science, rich in things, yet our time is fractured at the point of the meaning of life itself, because the fear of death has become so irrational. But it doesn't have to be that way. We can face reality with courage and understanding. We can reduce anxiety by learning to cope with competence and honesty with all of life, the tragic as well as the joyous. We can have true inner creativity if only we will face ourselves and our fears, and work to resolve them with the skill and courage we have been able to show in other realms of modern life.

To that end I invite you to become a committee of one to face the critical problems of escape from reality and anxiety about death by examining your own basic philosophy, by becoming acquainted with the basic facts as present research makes them available, and, finally, by starting a new and wiser educational approach with children, so that they need not enter the future with irrational fear and anxiety but may rather develop a wise and sound philosophy of both life and death.